"This poetry collection is driven by the strong voice of a mature poet who has come to terms with the unexpected twists and turns of her life's journey. It is the voice of loss and love, longing and forgiveness, pain and joy. Ultimately, it is the voice and mind and heart celebrating survival and self-determination. It is the voice of a woman of endurance."

Dhalma Llanos-Figueroa, Novelist-Essayist
Daughters of the Stone / A Woman of Endurance

Meditation on Love, Dancing, Loss, and Forgiveness

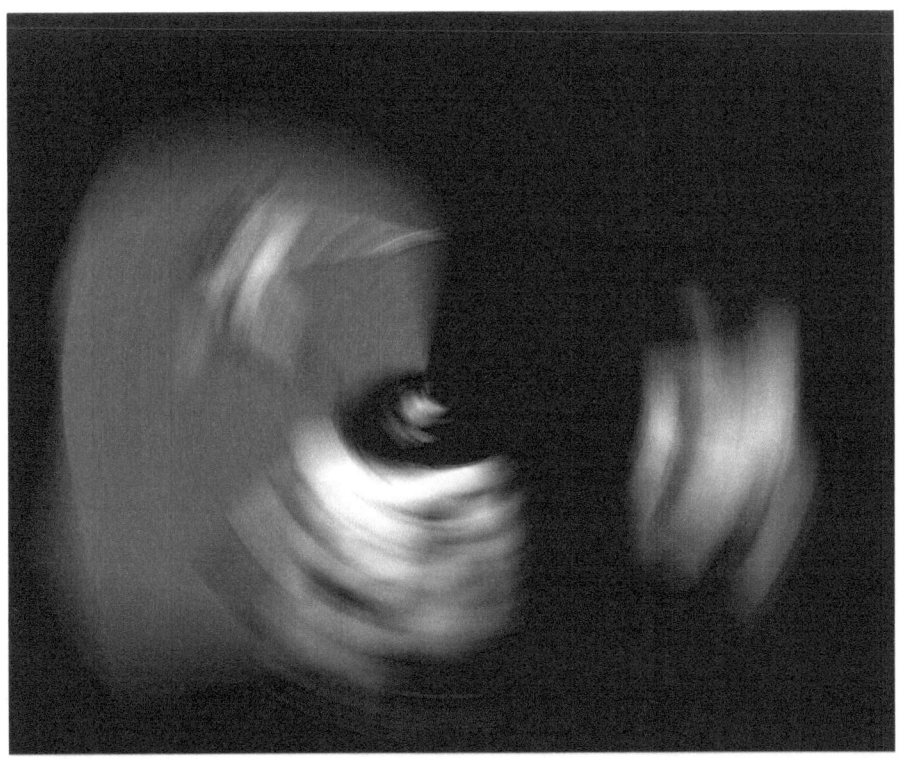

Meditation on Love, Dancing, Loss, and Forgiveness © Carmen Bardeguez Brown 2021
All rights reserved, **Marrowstone Press**
ISBN: 978-0-578-32548-4

notes: "Adiós" was published in the anthology Horatio 2 edited by Elaine Sexton.

Cover /interior artwork by Galen Garwood © *2021*

Meditation on Love, Dancing, Loss, and Forgiveness

by
Carmen Bardeguez Brown

Marrowstone Press

TABLE OF CONTENTS

I

Introduction   i
Heart Strings   1
Concierto   2
Surviving Raul   3
Waves   5
Adiós   6
In Search of Answers   7
Infinity   9
Nothing but Motion   10
Destino   11
Wonder   12
At This Moment   13
Cosmic Reality / Realidades Universales   15
Cenizas   16
Physics   17
God's Particle   18
Beloved   19
Despertar   20

II

A Year and a Half after Raul's Passing   23
La promesa del bailador   26
Hoy aprendi a bailar el vals   27
Waltz I II III   28
Dancing Night   30
Dancing Mantra   31
Tango   32
Tango Argentino   33

Learning How to Dance   34

Conversaciones de un sábado por la tarde en Casa Amadeo   35

Dance Conversations II   36

Dancing Steps   38

Dancing Steps: The Follower Leads   39

Conversation Between the Leader and the Follower   40

Friday Night   43

Salsa Dancer   45

Bachata del olvido   46

Vámonos Pal' Monte   47

El Son del Trucuta   48

Maestro   49

Mario   53

My First Dances   55

Mario   56

Mami   58

Mami I   59

Memoria   61

Voice Mail   62

Eres feliz   63

Can I see another's woe
And not be in sorrow too?
Can I see another's grief
And not seek for kind relief?

from William Blake's On Another's Sorrow

Introduction

We live and we die.

That is just the way it is. Once our biological body expires, our soul leaves this dimension and moves on to mysterious dwellings. Mortals don't have access to the other side of the veil of existence. Ancient spiritual traditions have documented how it must be, or how we expect it to be, depending on the maturity, development, and compassion of our souls. But we really don't know. All we know is that when someone that we love crosses the pathway to the spirit world, our existence on this side of the veil is shattered. We lose our sense of identity.

We know that we all eventually will die but never discuss it. It's interesting that one of the most mysterious moments of human existence is seldom discussed in the Western World, at least in modern times.

Poetry is my life compass. In the last few years, I've lost so many people I love. They are on the other side of the veil. They only exist now in memories and dreams. Sometimes I feel them close, very close, almost like a whisper. A few times, I have listened to their words of wisdom as memories, consolations in my journey through grief.

There is life after physical death. We just don't know exactly how it is. But I can certainly feel the loved ones' support on my path to recreate myself with an identity that embraces the suffering and loss. Love is a real energetic force, and it never ends. It just is. After six years of mourning and going through the most difficult phases of grief, I can say that our lives are measured by the amount of love we give and allow ourselves to receive. Compassion towards ourselves and others decides our fate on this journey. A life lived with passion and love is revealed in those last breaths.

This is my humble way to share how using poetry, learning, and practicing mindfulness meditation, ballroom dancing, and forgiveness have allowed me to navigate the spiritual, emotional, and physical journey of grief.

I hope that these poems touch your heart and allow it to be open to the experience of deep love, because it is only through love that you can experience and understand the mysterious goodbye of grief and mourning.

My mother passed away during her sleep in May 2021. It has been a little over a month. I received her ashes from the funeral home on Monday. Mami was 94 and had a full life. She always told me how she was thankful for the life she had including some of the sinsabores. She had such a zest for life and an imposing personality and character. She loved Puerto Rico and refused to live anywhere else. Mami never recuperated from losing two daughters, my younger sister succumbed to cancer, and my oldest sister lost her battle to Alzheimer's.

Mami told me as a matter of fact that she was ready to go to live with God. She was ready. She said that she already was done here, and she told me she loved me and thanked me for what I had done for her and my sisters.

Her preparation and my acceptance don't make it any easier, but I guess it was less traumatic. Losing your mother leaves you at times lost in ways that are indescribable.

Now, I must figure out my way in this world and reconfigure my identity as an older and still productive person in this ever-changing world. Mami embarked on a new journey; so have I.

Carmen Bardeguez-Brown
Chiang Mai, Thailand
June 2021

"Looking deeply, we should also see that there is no birth, there is no death; there is no coming, there is no going; there is no being, there is no non-being; there is no same, there is no different."

Thich Nhat Hahn

Part I

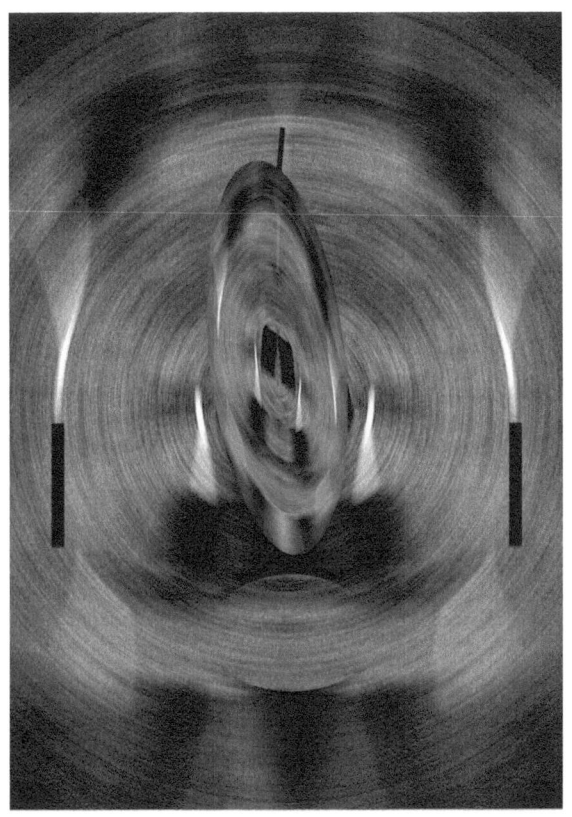

"The wound is the place where the light enters you."
Rumi

I have a journey that takes a long time,
Along a distant path.

Exert Gitimalya #14
Tagore

Heart Strings

My heart is shattered in pieces but it's not dead.
It has deep scars
as wide as valleys
wounds as deep as the crevices at the bottom of the sea.

I am sewing pieces
bleeding
sorrow
pain
suffering
loss.
My heart is raw.

I am carving a
musical instrument
with pieces of my soul.

Sounds
melodies
pulsating
dancing
like the nightingale
on a moonless night.

Compassion and wonder
slowly mending my heart.

Concierto

We are musical notes
vibrating.
Luminous energy
dancing
playing
in
the
orchestra
of
creation.

Surviving Raul

I felt a cold breeze in my heart. Doctors were not telling me what was wrong. Nobody knew. Everyone seemed to be confused in the ER. I just noticed how your breath was quickly leaving you. You wanted to talk but could only mumble a few words. My heart succumbed to quiet despair. My son, a spiritual warrior, knew what I did not want to face: you were going to leave us.

I think at that moment my soul started to break into pieces.

I was driving behind the ambulance, stunned, begging God to heal you. It was at that moment of vulnerability and fear that I saw light yellow butterflies dancing in front of the car. Suddenly, I experienced a calmness that only Spirit can give. Now, every time I see light yellow butterflies, I feel Spirit and feel your love.

God-Spirit uses nature to remind us of our spiritual connection. Those butterflies were sent to remind me that we are not alone, not even in our darkest times. Now, I notice yellow butterflies every time that I need a reminder of my spiritual connection to God-Spirit.

We had planned the vacation for months. We were so excited about going to Santa Fe and then to San Antonio to visit your brother. But life had other plans for both of us. This was going to be a one way ticket for you, my love. You were going to start a journey into eternity, into other realms of existence which are still a mysteries for those of us on the other side of the veil. I was going to be left alone.

I miss you.

Raul, I miss saying your name.

I don't hear your wise comments about life and the simplicity of country living in Puerto Rico. Your stories about life as a poor, happy kid in Guayama. Your adventures and travesuras with your friends, finding ways to play with whatever you could find. Like when you went to the river looking for jueyes and cocolías to eat. I never got tired of listening to the nicknames people in your barrio had for colorful neighbors like Juan el cojo, Juana la puta, or María la tuerta.

I felt the love that you had for your grandmother, Mami Pancha. I vividly recall the tender way you described how much you loved going to the monte near her house to get her oregano brujo. The way you described how the monte was covered with the dark green herb and how the rich, pungent aroma made you happy.

I know that she received you with open arms when you arrived at your new home.

You and I loved gardening and dreamed of getting a farm when I retired, but that dream is no more.

Sometimes I feel you, a feeling that evokes in me a deep, strong pleasure that engulfs my entire body. You had such beautiful brown skin. I loved to touch and caress your nose and canela lips. I miss rolling to your side of the bed and placing my head on your chest and feeling protected. Those intimate moments made me feel complete and whole. Nothing could happen to me because you held me.

I always thought that with you, I could face anything.

I miss your silly jokes and melodic voice. You would sing boleros anywhere, whether we were alone or in the supermarket or just walking in the streets. Singing helped you cope with your sadness and the pain of losing your sight in the prime of your life. You embraced the pain, but you never allowed it to define you.

I still have the many love notes you sent me that melted my heart. I loved writing you my special poems … just for you. I loved awaiting your feedback. Your usual, "Hmm interesante." You always understood me in so many ways.

Before you left, you kept insisting that I should complete my two novels.

You were my soulmate. We loved and lived in the present moments of silent "te quieros".

Raul, our love has helped me navigate the transition of your earthly departure. God is slowly helping me start a new beginning. I'm walking slowly. Like a newborn, my steps are eager and adventurous, but I'm also very cautious and mindful.

I have tried to create a new life but it's hard. I know that you want me to live and I promise, my love, that I will. That until the day we see each other again, I will live my life fearlessly with integrity and passion. That I will do what I love and is in my heart. I will face the universal canvas of infinite possibilities and trust God to guide me. A new song will be born in my soul. A mended heart will help me navigate this new journey.

This, my loving Raul, is the best way I can honor our love.

Waves

No coming no going
that is what Thich Nhat Hanh says.
Like the ocean and the waves
all are one and the same.

No coming no going
like the movement of our hearts
beating
one-two
one-two-three
one
two.

No coming no going
our bodies
dancing.
Waves in the ocean
Synchronicity of rhythms
love and belonging.

No coming no going
waves.
No coming no going
ocean.
No coming no going
waves in the ocean
dancing
together forever
as
one.

Adiós
> *For Raul*

Of crimson lips with the coconut scent
of Spanish ballads you loved to sing at the end of the day.
Of your boring jokes and your unique frown
the laughs we shared, warm hugs and more.
Of that which is memorable
of your life force dancing
in truncated syllables.
Demised... approaching
like fire melting away regrets and "te quieros".
Of that which is passion
of that
of the sound of your silence.
Of your sweet guayaba kisses
ebbing.
navigating the unknown
of that journey, my love.
Of that.

In Search of Answers

On July 4, Juno made it to Jupiter
named after the Roman god of war
protector of the empire
suitable name for a NASA spacecraft.

Her eyes will show us a world
that possibly adds more questions
about our own existence.

Unique images will disturb scientific dogma
questions answered with more questions
&
I am
here.
Trying to understand
painful transitions of the human fate
my husband's sudden death
& now
I am a witness to my young sister's denial of her impending demise.
She clings to life as fiercely as she can like a hyena feasting on her last meal.
She struggles to find peace
but
aren't we all?
Afraid to leave what we know and love to face the unknown?
My older sister is losing her mind
in the tragic universe of Alzheimer's & a life wasted in fear and depression.
&
I
wonder
what is life?
What connects this web of memories, experiences, feelings, and emotions?
Daily rituals
conversaciones
palabras
abrazos
regrets
te quieros
& silence.

Silencio
Always
el maldito
inevitable
silencio.

Why am I fascinated by Juno's voyage?
While I
helplessly
see loved ones depart
facing new realities.
Going into worlds I do not understand.

I
like Juno
witness wonders
tapestries
of
images and sounds
journeying
into the unknown.

Infinity

for Hector and Anddy

There is no coming
there is no going.
We dance in the moment.
We breathe and manifest.
There is no coming
there is no going.
Our souls twirl and pivot
musical notes
dancing.
There is no coming
there is no going.
For a moment we manifest
for a moment we dance
& love
& and love again.

Inspired by the words and work of Zen master Thich Nhat Hanh.

Nothing but Motion

for Dewey B. Larson and Einstein

Nothing but motion
like the Caribbean blue palettes of a clear summer sky.
Birds singing
flowers kissing
dancing bees
reciprocal relation.

Like stars
sending us their glittering smile through eons of time
past
present
future.
Floating
in a sea of darkness.

Like the dust of the cosmos bathing our skin
your smile
my giggles
our souls
dancing.

The universe bathes us in cosmic light.
Waves and photons dancing in galactic explosions.
We dream in rhythms
breathing
wake up
from the chrysalis seeded in the sky.
Chirping like baby birds
Our existence
$E = mc^2$
The wind in our skin
wondering
why
& then
fly.

Destino

Siento como que el viento de la noche lentamente se lleva a mis hermanas.

Presagio
muerte
corazón contrito
pena
pena
y no sé
y trato de entender
vida
vida.

¿Qué eres tú y por qué transformas nuestra esencia?

Incomprensión eterna
pena
pena
escucha mis palabras.

¡Vida!

Hazme entender
el porqué de nuestra existencia
pena
pena
muerte
eterna.

Wonder

At this moment

A star says her last goodbyes
an old couple kisses as they walk the promenade
a crying child is console by her mother
a soldier follows orders, and his soul is lost in a lifetime of regrets
the Amazon is gasping for air
strange airplanes navigate our skies
dolphins talk to each other
an orchid blooms
a river burns in methane
a father hugs his son
a sad young man plays guitar in the park
cloud formations dance in the skies
We hear strange sounds
our cells die a silent death
millions of cells are born
We hear laughter in playgrounds.

At this moment

Lovers live a lie
galaxies collide
bread is bake in a brick oven
we forget who we are
plants give
us oxygen
conflicting emotions hijack our thoughts
we think we are different
politicians are corporate puppets
lovers' hearts dance
another black man is shot.

At this moment

We have the largest incarcerated population in the world
Oscar López-Rivera (*), Mumia Abu Jamal and Leonard Peltier rot in prison for believing in justice
& a more equal love.

At this moment

Someone says I love you while loving someone else
I search for answers
I ask questions
I cry for you.

At this moment

I give anything to kiss you & hear your voice
loneliness is our faithful companion
&
I
we
wonder what is life?

At this moment

Someone is raped
silence is loud
students don't learn
monastics chant
hunger claims millions
a newborn opens her eyes
a dancer waltz in a small city plaza
another child drowns in an ocean of indifference.

At this moment

Earth travels around the sun
the universe expands
death is the beginning of life
pain is all I know
injustice engulfs our existence
we succumb to fear.

At this moment

We forget to love
someone realizes that we are all one.

At this moment

I close my eyes
I notice my breathing
now
is
possible.

At this moment

Two souls are one
wonder is miracle
we are cosmic dust
imagination is life
impermanence is real
hearts beat
breathe
hearts
beating
beating
we
breathe
hearts beating
&
I
we
breathe
in
awe.

*Oscar Lopez-Rivera was pardoned by President Barack Obama in January 2017.

Cosmic Reality
Realidades Universales

One
I
kiss you.

Two
We are photons of love

Tres
Somos luces eternas
que resplandecen
en el umbral
del deseo.

Cenizas

Llegaste a este país
pero no saliste de él
el tiempo te atrapó
y la vida te engañó
pensaste en volver a tu islita
pensaste en el mar
y las palmeras
la brisa del Caribe en tus mejillas
y el sol del trópico en tu piel
marchita.

Fueron muchas las promesas
fueron muchas las mentiras
en un día de lluvia fría
tu corazón
explotó de pena.

El tiempo te atrapó
en este país
y no pudiste volver a tu
isla de palmeras.

El ocaso te llevó
entre quebrantos y penas
las cenizas de lo que fue tu vida
partirán algún día
a buscar el sol de tu islita
el sol de tu islita bella.

Te fuiste buscando una salida
te fuiste buscando una esperanza
las palmeras las cambiaste por concreto
y el calor por el frío intenso.

Y ahora tus cenizas embriagadas con mi pena
buscarán apacentamiento
en tu islita
en tu islita caribeña.

*The poem should be read with the cadence of a Bolero song

Physics

We are engaged in a quantum entanglement
heart to heart
love to joy
and then
no more.

God's Particle

Scientists discovered the Higgs boson particle
Are the mysteries of creation confirmed?
What we knew
what we now know
is that all?
about energy
about love?

Beloved

I know you
I know when you are near
how you caress
and seduce
the ones that cross your mystery.

Beloved
I have escaped your loving arms
but I know that when I least expect it
we will dance.
You take everything and leave nothing but a memory.

Beloved
our encounter
is inevitable
at any moment
in myriad ways
your love will seduce our senses
and steal our hearts.

Beloved
you are what you are
many names
celebrate your experience.
Anubis, Osiris, Ishtar, Kali
Thatanos, Mara, Cihuateteo
The Reaper
La Muerte.
Our destiny is sealed in your love.

Oh dear!
You take us to unknown
mysterious
worlds.

Beloved
we are scared (of you)
but know that
in the end
we are yours.

Despertar

Confieso que he vivido en penumbras
neblina de caprichos y sueños inertes de sombras
confieso que perdí la luna en un atardecer de diciembre
y no supe encontrar la sonrisa perdida de un niño jugando con las amapolas
y confieso que me gusta sentir el calor del sol quemar mi piel
mientras juego al esconder con los lagartijos y lagartijas
y sé que se me hace tarde porque el otoño se acerca
y que la pasión se apagó en la encrucijada de primavera
y es así que confieso
que no soy lo que escuché en una canción de juventud y anhelos
mas aquí estoy
con puño y letra
sudor y cicatrices
y el alma abierta.

Y es ahora que mi corazón palpita
y es ahora que mi corazón se alegra
buscando alforjas y golondrinas
buscando en papel rojo y orquídeas de seda
caminando hacia el infinito con las estrellas
sintiendo el polvo cósmico en mi respirar
mientras medito con las mariposas, los querubines, y el gato negro que encontré en la esquina del olvido.

Y aquí me tienes despertando.

Confesando mis travesuras con el pelo enriscado y rutas de plata en mi cabello que nacieron cuando le robé al pirata español sus leyendas.

¡Ay! ¿Pero qué será de mí despertando en el atardecer,
cómo encontraré el mapa
que me lleve a los misterios del universo?
¿Quién me acompañará en mis travesías y aventuras de colibrí?
¿Quién cantará conmigo el canto de las sirenas?
Mas confieso que el temblor que siento se despeja con el calor de las estrellas
las constelaciones me mandan telegramas y textos de amor y comedias
para reírme de los caprichos de esta vida pasajera.

II

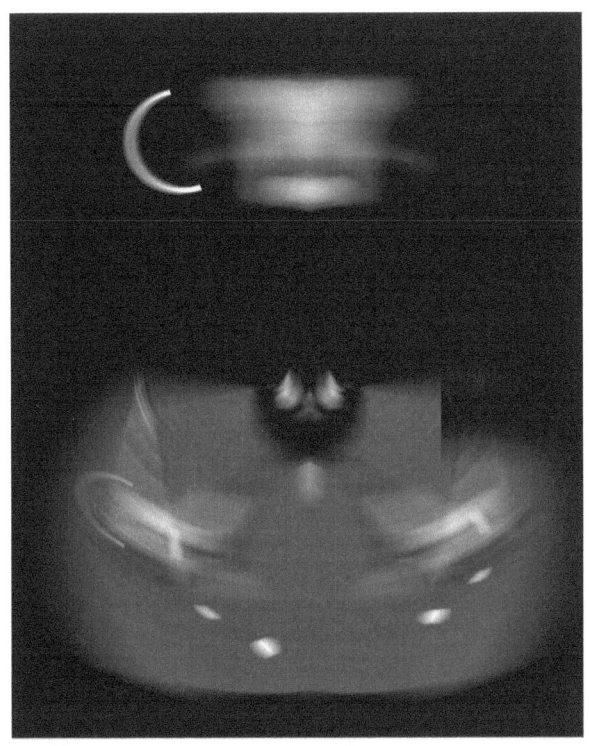

"Respond to every call that excites your spirit."

Rumi

"You were wild once. Don't let them tame you."

Isadora Duncan

"Why should I go from door to door in my false search?
The path itself shows me the path I have to follow.
I have come to know that this is the heart of the matter."

Garland of Songs 62
Gitimalya
Tagore

A year and a half after Raul's passing, I decided to enroll in ballroom dancing classes. I had been encouraging my late husband to take them with me, but his sudden death ended that dream. One day at work, I saw a dance performance by a resident teacher with her students. Watching them rekindled my desire to follow up with my dream of taking dance classes.

The first problem was to find a studio. Where could I go to learn how to dance tango and mambo like Rita Moreno in West Side Story? Towards the end of a long workday, Bibi, who was working as the Morris Campus records keeper, brought me an old book from the high school. She knew that I like to look at the yearbooks and artifacts my school was safeguarding on behalf of the campus.

As I browsed through one of them, I saw the name Arthur Murray; he was an alumnus of Morris High School. I took that as a sign and looked up the Arthur Murray Dance Studio near my home in Yonkers, New York. That was in December of 2016. I finally stepped into the studio in July of that year.

I was overwhelmed trying to balance my work, attending bereavement meetings, and supporting my younger sister who had terminal cancer, as well as my oldest sister who had an onset of early Alzheimer's. It was exceedingly difficult because both were in a state of denial. I responded by practicing mindfulness, developing new habits, and going regularly to Blue Cliff monastery. For almost two years they were my Shanga.

Mindfulness practice changed my life, but I needed more.

I wanted to experience joy to balance out the grieving while supporting loved ones who were at the end of their earth journeys. My role as a caregiver for my two sisters was taking a toll on my mental and emotional health. I couldn't even grieve the sudden death of my husband. I needed to do something about the energy of suffering and sadness that was in my physical body. Suffering and grief are not just emotional and spiritual processes; they are also a physical experience. There are empty spaces, sounds that you will never hear again, hugs and kisses that you will never receive. It is a physical pain.

Music and dancing help me connect to the rhythm of life. Afro-Cuban and salsa music are a powerful aspect of my identity and my poetry. My family loved music, and I was raised during the classic salsa period. I'm from a home where mami played everything from Charlie Palmieri, Johnny Pacheco, Ismael Rivera, Eartha Kitt, Nancy Wilson, Chuck Berry, Willie Colón, Orquesta Aragón, to The Jackson 5. At family gatherings during my entire youth, music played a vital role. Even during my high school dance parties, live salsa orchestras played.

On a hot July afternoon in 2016, my dream became a reality at The Arthur Murray Dance Studio in Yonkers. A new stage of my grieving process was transformed by the beauty of ballroom dancing and the beautiful relationship that evolved with teachers Mario and Bo and the studio owner, Lillian

I also took my older sister to the studio to take a few lessons with my teacher. She loved dancing and I wanted to give her an experience of joy and happiness, even if she would soon forget it. My teacher and the owner of the studio gave us that gift. Lillian told me to bring her as often as I could. My sister was happy. To my surprise, she remembered most of it until she couldn't anymore.

Around that time, I also discovered a cultural golden nugget at Bronx Music Heritage Center (BMHC) founded by maestro, bandleader-conductor, and professor Bobby Sanabria, along with his wife, the accomplished ethno-urban anthropologist, Elena Martinez. They represent the best of what cultural icons should be. They're successful in their professions and work diligently to preserve and expand the historical and current contributions of the musical history of the South Bronx. Their institution provides a calendar of yearly events and interactive workshops that increase awareness of the richness of Bronx musical history and the expansive creativity of the people of The Bronx.

The second phase of my grieving process or journey can be summarized as my willingness to open myself to live and give myself permission to experience joy while simultaneously navigating the different stages of grief and grieving.

I learned to dance Argentinian Tango, Waltz, Rumba, Mambo, Cha-Cha, Foxtrot, Kizomba, Bolero, and Paso Doble. My teachers taught me the intricacies of ballroom choreography. I laughed with my teachers and loved participating in showcases that forced me to learn the choreography they created for me. What a gift! I will never forget this experience.

Ballroom dancing helped me tap into unknown aspects of myself, as well as giving me the confidence to say to life: I am here! Alive and ready to wear my emotional scars like golden medallions.

Dancing taught me that grief and mourning are physical, emotional, and spiritual processes. My teacher Mario taught me that I needed to surrender to the sad notes of a bolero and embrace the sensuality of my body when I danced a Rumba, Mambo, or Salsa. Bo taught me to enjoy my body while dancing Tango and Kizomba. They both taught me to live in the moment.

La promesa del bailador

Te sigo como el marullo sigue a las olas
la brisa caliente al día afanoso
la tierna fruta a la semilla
tus besos en mis labios
y el calor de tu amor en mi piel
tus pasos
tu ritmo
tus caderas
las tengo en mi compás
y bailamos
navegando mapas de territorios escondidos
tesoros envueltos en algas y corales rojos.

Te sigo como el deseo sigue la pasión
la luz a la sombra
el llanto a la sonrisa
y el paladar de tus caricias en mi corazón.

Te sigo como los planetas siguen a las estrellas
el cometa a su destino
los pasos al camino
y tu cintura en mis manos.
Bailamos sedientos
buscando el oasis
éxtasis
en el baile.

Te sigo como la abeja busca a la flor
embriagado en tu esencia
eres capullo delicado
que se abre en el vaivén del son
y bailamos
unidos
siguiendo nuestro ritmo.

Hoy aprendi a bailar el vals

El vals es similar a las olas del océano

los pasos son melódicos

armoniosos

vienen y van

vienen y van

despacios

y melódicos

vienen y van

vienen y van

escucha el palpitar de las olas

y sabrás lo que te estoy diciendo.

Siente la suavidad

las olas

deja que tu cuerpo sea uno con el océano

las olas

escucha

despacio

el vals

la música

siente la armonía en tu cuerpo

las olas

los pasos

vienen y van

vienen y van

el vals.

Waltz I II III

I
Hummingbirds in your skin
sacred mantras in your arms

II
Surrender

2 3 4
1 5 6

My heart

2 3 4
1 5 6

Bleeds

2 3 4
1 5 6

Lead me to dreams
of buried magnolias.

2 3 4
1 5 6

My heart

2 3 4
1 5 6

You

2 3 4
1 5 6

at last.

III

Simplicity of movement
graceful mantra of love.

Dancing Night

Dancing the night away

in steps of forgiveness and joy

crimson lips

sucking air

contortions

movements

desires

steps

step

step

step

leave it on the floor

steps

steps

move your hips

once more

feel the rhythm

feel your soul

move your hips just once more

this is your life

this is your moment

transform your sorrow into blissful joy.

Dancing Mantra

Breathing in
I know I am breathing in.
Breathing out
I dance.

Breathing in
I know I am breathing in.
Breathing out
I am free.

Breathing in
I know I am breathing in.
Breathing out
I dance.

Breathing in
I know I am breathing in.
Breathing out
I am free.

Breathing in
I know I am breathing in.
Breathing out
I dance.

Breathing in
I know I am breathing in.
Breathing out
I am free.

Tango

En tus brazos
siento el latido de mi ser
me dejo llevar por la pasión
la suavidad
y en un momento
los pasos
del ocho son uno
tu cuerpo y mi cuerpo
bailando
sintiendo a Gardel
la música de corazón a corazón.

Tango Argentino
> *For Bo*

Comienza con el cabeceo
y aceptando la tanda
nuestros cuerpos ondean deseos
la mirada esquiva sigue pasos cual pantera buscando su presa
en tus brazos nuestros latidos
cadencia
caricias
un abrazo perfecto
las piernas entrelazadas 2-4
4-4
escuchando la voz de Gardel improvisando
un baile de más de cien años
Piazzola
Sarli
lamento y nostalgia
cantado con bandoneón
nos dejamos llevar por la pasión.
los ganchos y contra giros
el ocho y el ocho cortado molinete con sacadas carrusel de un sólo cuerpo
nuestro silencio
mirada firme
enganche
entrada
al compás
castigada
latigazo
latigo fuerte
bailando canyengue
los pasos de cangrejo y candomblé secretos de historias escondidas en arrabales y milongas de Azabache.

Learning How to Dance

One

Dancing is...
listening
to your body temple
choreography of rhythms
music
and
balance.
Breathing love
and
coordination.

Two

Dancing is...
knowing that you are free
in every breath
in every step.

Conversaciones de un sábado por la tarde en Casa Amadeo
Para Mario

Entre el pasado y la curiosidad del presente
las palabras se salpican de ilusión
de sueños y canciones
música creada en la pasión del corazón.
Tus latidos
los escucho en mi suspirar.
Boleros y Rumba
Salsa y Guaguancó
se entrelazan en
experiencias cosechadas en palabras
semillas de esperanza.
Conversaciones
deseos de crear y ser creado.
Composiciones
y
tu voz
gimiendo canciones
que necesitan salir de tu corazón
pensamientos de almas unidas
en la eternidad
música nacida en el umbral de la conversación.

Dance Conversations II
    Inspired by "Dance Etiquette" by Mario Moreta

You say that I dance because it gives me a feeling of youth and sexiness. That is right, but what if I tell you that I also dance because I want to feel my spirit? That I dance because I am a wild goddess who enjoys herself moving under the light of a full moon while nymphs and she-wolves drum the music to the beat of the singing stars.

I agree that dancing is a feeling you can't find anywhere. The only thing close to it is multiple orgasms.

Hmm... so men are supposed to help me fulfill that experience through dance? What if I tell you that it is the other way around? Men are captivated by our curves and mystery, and it is our sensual spell that entices them to help us navigate ecstasy through dance.

I love the way in which you describe the process of asking and the gentle manners of chivalry before the dance experience. It is a kind of foreplay before the sexual act.

You say that we relate dancing to sex, and I say of course. Then again, could it be that we are both searching for a spiritual experience?

I love to follow (at least in ballroom dancing) a partner that is a strong and gentle lead. No arguments there.

The end of a dance routine is a moment of sudden death. If you reach ecstasy with your partner, you suddenly feel the happiness and sadness of departure. I agree with you that the beginning of a dance experience and the moment of goodbye are as important as the physical and spiritual experience of the actual dance.

Touching is so personal and spiritual and we sometimes forget how sacred that is. When we touch, we exchange energy. When we dance, we exchange love for the dance, and if we acknowledge how sacred that experience is, we can realize that dance is a gift of the gods.

Thank you, Mr. Moreta, for an interesting conversation.

Dancing Steps

The Follower

In the moment
Waves
Sounds
Rhythm
m
u
s
i
c

response
response

Anticipation
response

Listen to the love notes
Pasión
Suavidad
Candor
Communication of souls

response
response

unidos
como una canción.

Dancing Steps: The Follower Leads...

Inspired by Patty Contenta

Caderas
deseo
secreto de mujer
esencia como canela
despacito
con ritmo
embriágalo como la miel seduce a la abeja.

Síguelo
llénate de él
siéntelo en tu ser.

Baila
suave y despacito.

Mueve las caderas
siente el ritmo.

Déjale saber que tú le escuchas
trastorna sus sentidos
embriágalo
embrújalo.
Despacito y con ritmo.
Despacito y con ritmo.

Déjale saber que él puede tocar tus deseos
despacito y con ritmo.
Despacito
con ritmo
con ritmo.

Conversation Between the Leader and the Follower

Inspired by Daniel Heroux

I was told
that I can only feel when I dance
I cannot think nor say with words
emotions that arise in my skin when I touch you.
I was told
I should feel my body.
Let your movement guide my steps.
Desires "a flor de piel".
What do you think?
You lead me to places
buried in my skin.
I
follow your contortions
panther-like steps
Matador
take me
otra vez
slowly
slowly
fast
slowly
slowly
fast
then…we breathe each other's breath
dancing steps on fire.
I
just follow
I
just follow
feel
primal desires
dancing steps on fire.

Make me feel
Matador
you are my lead.
Take me pantera
to nirvana
buscando devorar
mis deseos
bailando
I will push you with my passion
slowly
slowly
fast
slowly
slowly
fast
I
just follow
I
just follow.
Make me feel
your lead
Matador
dance with me
fast
slowly
fast.
We are
dancing with fire
our bodies
waves
rhythm of emotions

slowly
slowly
fast
slowly
slowly
fast
feel
lead
feel
lead
feel
Primal desires
caressing
my
skin
Matador
lead me
slowly
fast
lead me
slowly
fast.
Make me
feel
again
one
more
time.

Friday Night

Bailando
tocando
sintiendo
rumbeando
candela con candela
caderas
muslos
piernas

Elixir
de
tambores
saciando
venas

Orgia de ritmos

gimiendo
placer de la piel
bailando

Cuerpos rumbeando

Cuerpos
sudando

Bailando
tocando
tocando
CUERPOS
bailando
rumbeando
cuerpos tocando

rumbeando
tocando
bailando
tocando rumbeando
cuerpos
bailando
bailando
bailando
BAI LAN

Salsa Dancer

Eyes
transfixed
movements
possession
syncopate
contortions
sacred body meditation
Shangó's libations
blessings of the soul
timbales
Negrura
improvisation
conga
bongó
timbales
Candomblé
Plena.
Surrender to the temple
demigod of carnal desires
Caderas bathe in the Holy waters of Yemayá
electric arms
melodic legs
sensibilities sacrificed to the altar of creation
Bomba
Candomblé
Plena.
Orishas breathing fire
eruptions
    R
     i
      t
       u
        a
       l
       s
negrura
timbales
bongó.

Bachata del olvido

La noche está escondida
en el silencio de tu olvido
tu voz de ruiseñor
se apagó en la soledad
y el paso quebrantado
de este amor que vive en ruinas
lo dejo apacentado
en el vaivén del qué dirán.

Qué tristeza, Dios
qué tristeza
saber que este baile me hace recordarte más y más.

Caderas onduladas
gimen ritmos de agonía
brazos como alas
vuelan hacia el mar.

Qué tristeza, Dios
qué tristeza
tus caricias son mentiras
son mentiras
nada más.

Tus vueltas son cadenas
tus mentiras me encadenan
y así
bailando esta bachata
me refugio en el silencio de tu adiós.

Qué tristeza, Dios
qué tristeza
tus caricias son mentiras
y este baile incrementa mi agonía
de un amor de mentiras
de mentiras y nada más.

Qué tristeza, Dios
qué tristeza
saber que este baile me hace recordarte más y más.

Vámonos Pal' Monte

Para Papi

It was late afternoon and Papi went straight to the terrace
He got the LP from the bag and immediately powered on the turntable.

Papi smiled at me.
I had never seen him so excited about an LP
I wondered what magic sounds would come out of that record
He started mimicking sounds and with his hands made a sudden quick turn
towards me, and extended his right hand, inviting me to dance.

> Vámonos pal monte
> Vámonos pal monte
> Pal monte pa' guarachar
> Vámonos pal monte
> Que el monte me gusta más

Papi was smiling and I basked in his happiness.
It was one of the few precious moments that I saw him enjoying music and dancing.
For the first time I realized that Papi liked salsa
I always thought that he only liked boleros.
It was a perfect afternoon
Dancing with Papi and discovering that he was a salsero

El Son del Trucuta

Trucuta trucuta
    mue   veE te
   mue veE te
  tru cuta trucuta
sway
it
trucuta
trucuta
   spit IT
trucuta trucuta
      sTepS
trucuta trucuta
desires on fire

       Trucuta trucuta
       compás
trucuta trucuta
     vibrating
   trUcuta   trucUta
       Trucuta trucuta
    vibrating compás
Trucutu
tucutrA
sacred tingles
TRucutA
       RucutA
TrucutA
         RUCUTA
vibrating compás
trucuta trucuta
vibrating compás
trucuta tucutra
vibrating compás
trucuta trucuta
vibrating compás
TRUCUTA tracutra
vibrating
compás
vibrating compás
Trucuta.

Maestro

For Bobby Sanabria

Smoking Black suit cannot contain your
                                              S
                                          w
                                                  ing
 Deep
     deep
    deep
      Rhythms
   running
    through
   your skin
Master of Ancient contortions
     Scratching
        scat
        scat
Melodies
     crujiendo
Música
Ran can can
     timbales
    congas
 trumpets
&
 flutes
Dance at
      your Musical command.

Deep
  deep
    deep

Maestro
     Swirls
on the
Stage
pivots & jumping Swings
a la' Cab Calloway

Deepity dat
Deepity dat
    Trucutu
Trucutu
  Ca tan
que
   bueno
      está
sigue el Soneo
Maestro
  Ta ca tan
Ca tan.

Afro-Cuban chants
    Simmering from the band
Griot
 of
 HistorYcal renditions
    Orishas
dancing
al va y ven del Can Can

Clave
Dímelo
dímelo

Dímelo
mamá
suena ese cuero duro
una y otra vez más
levanta las voces del Triángulo
Del África
Pal' Caribe
y el norte
Ya tú sabes Papá.
Maestro
The Gods anointed your ears
your skin was bathed in the Rhythms
of the ancestors
&
today
You
   Swirl
Aché
for us to pray for redemption.

Trun ca ta
ca taN
Trun ca ta
ca taN
suéname
esa

Clave

suénamela
una vez más.

Trun ca ta
ca taN
Trun ca ta
ca taN
trompetas
conga
flauta
timbales
sonando el Aché
una vez más.

Maestro
  Our
musical priest
transforming
  pain
&
laughter
music
make us Holy
dan
    cing
 al

Compás.

Caderas
Muslos
    s
      t
        e
      p
      s
Caderas
Muslos
s
t
 e
p
s
contortion
of spirits
the Holy Ghost
    se
  me ne
        a
   In
every breath

   You
Master griot
musical Orisha of our souls
    Maestro Sanabria
Gracias
for your love
of the
Afro-Cuban son.

Mario

> "Forgiving does not erase the bitter past. A healed memory is not a deleted memory. Instead, forgiving what we cannot forget creates a new way to remember. We change the memory of our past into a hope for our future."
> *Louis B. Smedes*

> "To err is human, to forgive, divine."
> *Alexander Pope, An Essay on Criticism*

Mario Moreta was my dance teacher.

He came into my life at a time when I needed his love and support, and I came into his when he needed spiritual guidance. I danced with him for two years that felt like forever. Two souls in search of meaning learning that true friendship lives forever. He wrote me a poem, that he told me was the first he ever wrote. My heart received his words, and they started to melt the scars of grief and suffering after losing my husband.

I wrote him several poems that were inspired by our interaction during our two-year dance collaboration. He taught me dance through poetry and I taught him poetry through dance. I remembered how he told Patty Contenta, a world-class award-winning dancer and Arthur Murray coach, that he never had a student like me. He told me he had to be different when he explained the dance movements to me. I'm not entirely sure what he meant, but I still have the many recordings of his private lessons that show how he learned to be a poet while teaching me to dance.

For two years, Mario inspired me to write about my newfound love of ballroom dancing. We both knew how dance transformed our sadness into joy. We laughed and cried and talked and hugged. We thought that we would dance forever and compete at Arthur Murray competitions. We were planning and rehearsing to participate in a competition in Florida. We had routines for Cha-Cha, Mambo, Swing, Bolero, and Waltz.

Life had other plans for us.

A few days before his death, I told Mario that I was going to dedicate a section of the book to him about our friendship and about how dancing together guided me through the path of suffering, forgiveness, and love.

We loved each other and knew that our paths had crossed to enrich our lives. He died an untimely death under circumstances only God and destiny know. But yet again, who knows the real reason why we come into this life? Some souls manifest for a short time, and like a comet, burn fast.

I miss our weekly lunch dates where we brainstormed and co-wrote the studio newsletter, talked about life, music, love, and our dreams of dancing and competing. Mario was a passionate salsa dancer and as he used to say: "Un negrito que baila waltz". We knew that above all we were friends who supported each other's growth.

Forgiveness is the seed that allows love to flourish. Love never ends, love is eternal. The most perfect love is the one that God gave to us and through that love we learn to love ourselves, our children, spouses, families, and friends. God's love allows us to be compassionate and loving to every human and sentient being on Earth.

We need to love each other, every day. We need to support each other with kindness and empathy. Love heals. Love is the most powerful energy in the universe because it comes from creation, because it comes from God.

Mario's charisma and goodwill touched many. His love for dance and using it to heal was his earthly call. I know that he's dancing his way to Heaven. I know that God is guiding his dance steps forever.

My First Dances
To Carmen

I can't live without movement. Without my escape to be free. Dancing with a lady is everything to me. The feeling I get from the feeling I give; all I learn from my partner as I'm able to feel her life through her response.

I look at her eyes with a smile and show her that everything is okay. I hold her hand firmly to show her that the next four minutes are for us. Just us! I want you to be with me. I need you to be with me. Just for this song at least. Show me that we can share this moment where we don't give a fuck! Where we're stars, burning it up, shining amongst others. If people see us, who cares? I want them to see. The feelings I get from the feelings I give are the feelings we create. You don't have to dance like me to shine, just with me.

She's never danced like this before. She never thought she could. I could tell by how she responds to the turn. How she responds to my every movement. I like her dedication, but no. Take your time! Let me enjoy this dance with you. I don't care if you can turn. I don't care about what you know or how you look, I just want you to not give a fuck with me for the next three minutes.

I feel your strength when you're used to having to maintain your strong female image or your gentleness when life has abused your love. I understand. This is why I want you to dance with me. The feeling you get. Do you feel it with me? No! Don't think! Feel! That is the feeling you need. To forget about the past. Don't think about the future. Live in the gift of right now, the present.

Did you feel that? How did it feel? Be careful! It's like a drug. That feeling of getting lost in it. Getting lost in our bodies being in sync to the music. Your body looks amazing. How you're so sweaty and smell delicious.

Mario wrote this poem in October 2016. He told me he wanted me to read it in front of him because he wanted to see my reaction. I did and the rest as they say is history. I decided not to edit it and left it exactly as he wrote it for me.

Mario

I have to admit that what hurts most is not dancing with you.
I don't know what magic spell
incantation
your movements put on me.

You,
Devil of a dancer.
Dancing with you clouded my pretentious common sense.

I was transfixed
watching how you thrust your hips
while dancing rumba and cha-cha
or seeing the strength of your arms and legs
while you danced the paso doble.

Fierce Matador
pure fire on the dancefloor.

Your passionate teaching
your minute explanation of every detail of movement
enthralled me.
Your salsa dance bewitched me.

You allowed me to touch the musicality of your muscles
and the sincerity of your spirit
and I became your devout student.

You mesmerized and awakened my dreams of becoming
that which I always wanted.

Every turn you took awakened my body and soul.

Your love for dancing brought me to your knees.

And I
worship you like a god.
An angel
that came to rescue me from my sorrows.

But I can no longer
allow your fire to burn
my withered wings.

Because you see
I was once an angel
that forgot to fly
and you reminded me that I still had wings.
You reminded me that I must fly
that I too was born to dance.

I sent Mario this poem on August 4, 2018.
He responded with an email on the same day:
Amazing poem! You know, i read it and it reminds me of how similar we are, how compliments make us feel. As much as i act like I like it, the praise that i get from dancing, it still makes me feel weird. But I am happy for one thing. One goal! The one feeling that you've given me, that helps me wake up and have no problem doing this shit every day, for the rest of my life. And that's the transference of this gift. You have it now! you have made it your own. It's part of you and you of it. No matter what happens, please don't forget that this gift is about sharing. Never about keeping it to yourself. It's meant to inspire and appreciate. Remember that always!

Mami

I am still processing the loss of my mother. We both accepted that she was ready to embark on the long journey into the unknown. But you are never ready. As she bluntly asked me to never resuscitate her and told the attending doctor at the hospital in San Juan the same on Christmas Eve in 2020. She said, "Carmin I am ready to go I am done here. Estoy lista para irme con Dios." I guess if you are blessed of living a long life there comes a point when you say I'm ready for the next journey.

I was sad when she made that comment but also understood her decision and her stern audacity to continue to be honest till the end. Mami loved life and she was thankful for the many blessings and lessons that she had learned. She was a passionate woman. Loved her family, brothers and sisters and her beloved Puerto Rico. She also admitted that she never planned go live this long… she had lost many loved ones and her last years were full of suffering due to my sisters' lost battles with challenging diseases. She lived a full life and influenced many people as a daughter, sister, wife, mother, grandmother, aunt and teacher. She left a few written projects that I will try to complete in her memory like her collection of Puerto Rican sayings, many of which are becoming linguistically antiquated. She was a stern advocate of learning English as a Second language and not mixing it with her beloved Spanish. Mami also gave me the draft of a family memoir, and many pictures, including one of a distant cousin that died during the Normandy invasion on D-Day during World War II. She also loved books and instilled in me a loved for the written word. Above all, I inherited her passion and curiosity for life and her passion for learning about the influence of African culture in Puerto Rican culture. I have not lived in Puerto Rico in a long time but need to go back to spread her ashes on our beloved island.

You are never prepared to lose your mother.

Mami played a pivotal role in my life. Like her, I am a rebel and an adventure seeker. I am the dreamer of the family with a deep determination to be authentic. It is hard to write when you are grieving. I know that I need to get used to only hear her in my dreams.

Mami

Part 1

      I read the email a few times.
Dear Ms. Bardeguez-Brown we mail the remains of
What used to be Ms. Carmen L. Brown-Nieves.

We send it to the address you gave us in Tailandia.

  Tailandia sounds so foreign.

I could not grasp the meaning
    of
la que en vida fue

(The ephemeral mystery of life.)

No longer are
La que fue
    used to be

Bones and muscles
Eyes and organs turn into ashes.

No longer that voice to say te quiero
No longer the arms to hug you
Or the hands to kiss.

The I
no longer exist
(Who knows)?

Her face
(Appearing and reappearing)
An anecdote
Her voice
Pieces

of memories
running through my cheek
While
 a sudden wave of grief overtakes my entire body
Mami
    is no more.

Memoria

Parte 2

Y ahora
Ya no te llamo mas
Tengo la sortija que usabas y las llaves del apartamento
Tengo tu sonrisa y tu voz cicatrizadas en mi aliento
Ya no puedo decir mami
ya no puedo decir que volveré
y asi es la vida
un suspiro
ahora no se como quererte
y aun te sigo queriendo.

Voicemail

Todavía tengo tus mensajes en el teléfono
Y me hacen llorar.

Eres feliz

Cuando el viento te besa suavemente
y respiras profundamente
y notas el olor a grama fresca
y el ruiseñor cantando.
¿Eres feliz?

Cuando caminas lentamente
y ves el horizonte despejado
las montañas de color azul opaco onduladas
como mujer dormitando.
¿Eres feliz?

Cuando sientes lágrimas
recorrer memorias
y el corazón dormita en el pasado.
¿Eres feliz?

Cuando la luz del sol
calienta tu cuerpo
y quema los latidos de tu piel.
¿Eres feliz?

Cuando sabes que cada palpitar
te acerca más y más al ocaso.
¿Eres feliz,
eres feliz
eres feliz?

"Goodbyes are only for those who love with their eyes. Because for those who love with their heart and soul there is no such thing as a separation."

Rumi

Carmen Bardeguez-Brown is a Puertorican- Nuyorican poet. Her work is showcased in the documentary: Latino Poets in the United States by Ray Santiesteban. She has read at The Nuyorican Poets Café, The Fez, Mad Alex Foundation, Smoke, The Soho Arts Festival, Long wood Gallery, The Kitchen, The Bowery Poetry Club, The Boricua College Poetry Series, Governor Island poetry Festival, Harvard University,Bronx Music Heritage Center, Greenlight Bookstore, Se Buscan Poetas Poetry reading series and many other venues. Some of her work has been performed by Felipe Luciano's Poets' Choir and Butch Morris Conduction series.

Her work has been published by magazines such as: Tribes, Long Shot, 2 Horatio, Literary Anthology #1-3, School Voices, Long Shot, Fuse, Rutgers Gallery at New Brunswick, Phatitude Cultural Magazine, Woman Writers in Bloom on line magazine, La Pluma y La Tinta , Nuyorican Poets Writers Vol.1 edited by Dr. Nancy Mercado, Xanath Caraza Poetry Blog and On the Seawall. Her poems are in various anthologies such as: Aloud Voices from the Nuyorican, Manteca an Afro-Latino poems in the United States, I Can't Breathe, Musings in the time of the Pandemic, Straight from the Drums, Dreaming Rhythms: Despertando el Silencio and Al Otro lado del Mundo collaboration with JC Paz, Ghazal: Poetry like Bread International Video collaboration.

Ms. Bardeguez- Brown received the 2020 Latina 50 plus Literature Lifetime Award for her contributions to Latino Literature in New York.

www.ingramcontent.com/pod-product-compliance
Lightning Source LLC
Chambersburg PA
CBHW031301290426
44109CB00012B/670